From me to you. Let's talk about you.

You deserve all the best that life has to offer, and you have the ability to achieve it. As we all "Hammer Out a Living," I'd like to keep sharing tips and hear yours too.

Send me an email at karl@karldhughes.com to join the list and be part of the crew working on a successful life.

Hammering Out a Living

A Carpenter's Guide for a Successful Life

Karl D. Hughes

An Actionable Success Journal

E-mail: info@thinkaha.com
20660 Stevens Creek Blvd., Suite 210
Cupertino, CA 95014

Published by THiNKaha®
20660 Stevens Creek Blvd., Suite 210, Cupertino, CA 95014
http://thinkaha.com
E-mail: info@thinkaha.com

First Printing: June 2019
Hardcover ISBN: 978-1-61699-329-0   1-61699-329-4
Paperback ISBN: 978-1-61699-328-3   1-61699-328-6
eBook ISBN: 978-1-61699-330-6   1-61699-330-8
Place of Publication: Silicon Valley, California, USA
Paperback Library of Congress Number: 2019905303

Trademarks

All terms mentioned in this book that are known to be trademarks or service marks have been appropriately capitalized. Neither THiNKaha, nor any of its imprints, can attest to the accuracy of this information. Use of a term in this book should not be regarded as affecting the validity of any trademark or service mark.

Warning and Disclaimer

Every effort has been made to make this book as complete and as accurate as possible. The information provided is on an "as is" basis. The author(s), publisher, and their agents assume no responsibility for errors or omissions. Nor do they assume liability or responsibility to any person or entity with respect to any loss or damages arising from the use of information contained herein.

Acknowledgements

This is my first book. I know there will be more. I have to give credit where credit is due. No one can do it all, and it is usually true that many people are involved when something good occurs. There are always people who have helped out along the way, and I would like to acknowledge those who have helped me in this project.

First of all, I want to acknowledge the encouragement and guidance from the members of the New York City chapter of the National Speakers Association (nsanyc. org).

I am very grateful for the help from the team at AHAthat: Mitchell Levy, Jenilee Maniti, Hayley Cruz, and Nikka Ann Alejandro. They have been great in putting this all together.

I would simply not have been able to do this at all without the great advice and input from Noreen, Brendan, Derek, and Sue. Above all else, I am indebted forever to the most patient person I know. Without her, the book never happens: my wife, Pat Springsteen Hughes.

Thank you, Pat, I know I couldn't have done this without you.

Dedication

I have often wondered that if I ever wrote a book, to whom would I dedicate it.

A book of this nature is really a written version of a path that we, as tradesmen and tradeswomen, travel. So, the thought occurred to me to dedicate the book to those in the past who have taught us—those who learned and then passed on our trades and our traditions. They have given us the wisdom to earn a living with our hands, and they deserve our praise and our gratitude.

I would like to dedicate this book to all those who have worked with tools to provide for others. Their dedication and determination have served both those who hired them for their skills and the families and loved ones who benefited from their efforts. However, they should not remain anonymous. They are real people.

There is one in particular who provided me with a shining example of what it means to be a tradesman. He was someone who exemplified tenacity, determination, dedication, and love. His skills were excellent, and his approach to his work was with great purpose. It was often said of him that he got a lot of work done in a day.

I was blessed that he was the first carpenter that I worked with and the one who passed on to me all that it means to be a tradesman. For his own personal success, he had a plan, and in spite of starting out without a lot of education or money, he was able to become very successful! He managed to live that famous "American Dream" that is so often talked about.

That man was my dad, Hugh L. Hughes.

He was a carpenter, devoted husband, loving father, grandfather, and great-grandfather. He was a true friend and a man who lived with honor and dignity. His level of integrity and fairness was at the pinnacle of what military academies strive for.

He never gave up. Regardless of the struggles and challenges, he used all that he had to provide for those he loved. He loved his family unconditionally, worked tirelessly, and lived a life of integrity.

Much of what I share in this book can be attributed to the values that he lived by and the example he set. It is my sincere hope that others will appreciate his effort in life.

This book is dedicated to: Hugh L. Hughes, a man I am proud to say was my dad.

How to Read a THiNKaha® Book
A Note from the Publisher

The AHAthat/THiNKaha series is the CliffsNotes of the 21st century. These books are contextual in nature. Although the actual words won't change, their meaning will every time you read one as your context will change. Be ready, you will experience your own AHA moments as you read the AHA messages™ in this book. They are designed to be stand-alone actionable messages that will help you think about a project you're working on, an event, a sales deal, a personal issue, etc. differently. As you read this book, please think about the following:

1. It should only take 15–20 minutes to read this book the first time out. When you're reading, write in the underlined area one to three action items that resonate with you.
2. Mark your calendar to re-read this book again in 30 days.
3. Repeat step #1 and mark one to three more AHA messages that resonate. They will most likely be different than the first time. BTW: this is also a great time to reflect on the AHA messages that resonated with you during your last reading.

After reading a THiNKaha book, marking your AHA messages, re-reading it, and marking more AHA messages, you'll begin to see how these books contextually apply to you. AHAthat/THiNKaha books advocate for continuous, lifelong learning. They will help you transform your AHAs into actionable items with tangible results until you no longer have to say AHA to these moments—they'll become part of your daily practice as you continue to grow and learn.

Mitchell Levy, The AHA Guy at AHAthat
publisher@thinkaha.com

Contents

Foreword

March! Really, forward is such a great word. It is a word of action, and sometimes it is used as a command.

This book is meant for you, the working person, who spends a lot of time at their trade, who doesn't have a lot of time to read, but who wants to grow and succeed. We are not scholars—if we were, we'd have pursued that type of career. But we are "hands on" learners who want and need to hear the lessons of how to succeed at what we do.

This book has been intentionally set into a very simple format for a good reason. I don't want you to have to read pages and pages to understand these messages. Yes, I want you to go ahead and read the book, but I also want you to take action. I want you to think about the statements and ideas that are presented and then put as many of them to work for you as possible.

Read the book. Heed the call to action, and do all you can for yourself to build the life that you want to live.

Move forward. Forward at your own pace, with your own ideas and your own talent and determination. But always move forward—forward toward all that you hope for.

Introduction

I want you to live a better life.

I wrote this book specifically for my fellow carpenters, but also those in other blue-collar trades can greatly benefit from it. Just to keep things simple, if you are working in another trade, then simply insert your trade wherever it says carpenters, and it will pretty much have the same meaning.

In my forty-plus years in the construction industry, I have learned so many things that would have come in handy in my earlier years. I want to impart to you some of my experiences and the lessons I've learned, as well as tips and tricks on how you can live a better life.

In this book, you'll learn the importance of goal-setting, planning, and improving your skills and reputation as a tradesman or tradeswoman. You'll also learn how valuable money is and how you should carefully manage the money you earn today. All these things can help you lead a happy and successful life.

I have really great appendices in this book that tackle affirmations, important things not taught in school, qualities to build your reputation on, and short, quick tips from myself. If you have any tips or tricks that aren't in the book, please feel free to reach out to me so I can include them in future versions.

I want to help everyone, including those who are just starting and those who are already mid-way in their journey. May this book serve as a light to guide you on your path toward a successful life.

Karl D. Hughes

Every accomplishment starts with the decision to #TakeAction. Do you want to stay where you are now, or do you want to have a #SuccessfulLife?

Karl D. Hughes
http://aha.pub/ACarpentersGuide

Share the AHA messages from this book socially by going to
http://aha.pub/ACarpentersGuide.

Section I

Choosing Your Path

We often think about our future and the kind of life we would like to have. However, there are people who will impress upon us their own idea of success, like: "You need to go to school to get a decent job," or, "You need to be a doctor or a lawyer to be really successful."

Choosing our own path is challenging, especially if it's not what our family and friends expect from us. Always remember that our life is our own, and we're free to do what we want to do. We may face challenges but we can overcome them. What's important is that we're happy with the path we choose. The next thing to do is to take a step, and slowly but surely, that path will lead us to success.

One other thought : if you decide that you do not like this path, then remember that you are free to leave this path and choose another!

Watch this video:
http://aha.pub/ACarpentersGuideS1

1

The journey to a #SuccessfulLife starts with choosing a path. Follow your own path, not one chosen for you, and you're sure to have an awesome journey!

_____

_____

_____

2

Let go of other people's dreams and goals. You will have a #SuccessfulLife if you focus on your own goals and what you define as success.

_____

_____

_____

3

Don't feel bad for choosing a path that differs from other people's. You're responsible for your own happiness, not theirs. #SuccessfulLife

_____

_____

_____

4

Whatever you decide to do in your life and no matter what path you choose to follow, be sure it makes you happy. #SuccessfulLife

_____

_____

_____

5

There are many great careers, including the trades. Choose a profession that you like and always do your best to make it work for you. #SuccessfulLife

_____

_____

_____

6

No matter your path to success, you begin with a single step. Take action now! #SuccessfulLife

_____

_____

_____

7

Every accomplishment starts with the decision to #TakeAction. Do you want to stay where you are now, or do you want to have a #SuccessfulLife?

_____

_____

_____

8

The path you choose is yours and yours alone. Others may walk it with you, but no one can walk it for you. #TakeAction #SuccessfulLife

_____

_____

_____

9

Why wait for miracles to happen? Start working on yours today! #TakeAction #SuccessfulLife

_____

_____

_____

10

You may not need a college degree, but you do need an education. #SuccessfulLife.

_____

_____

_____

11

Your life doesn't begin in the future, it's already started. Choose your path now and live the life you want. #SuccessfulLife

_____

_____

_____

12

When you are ready to set your goals and start working on them, things will reveal themselves to you that you didn't see before. #SuccessfulLife

---

13

You have time to make things work and make things happen. You need to use it. #SuccessfulLife

---

14

You need to grow into a better person to be successful. Learn skills outside of your occupation, such as goal-setting and personal finance. #SuccessfulLife

_____

_____

_____

15

If you take a job that's been offered, even if not ideal, it can bring you to a better situation than where you'd be without it. #SuccessfulLife

_____

_____

_____

One way to make your day a good one is to start it off by saying, "Hey, let's begin the day on a positive note." #SuccessfulLife

Karl D. Hughes
http://aha.pub/ACarpentersGuide

Share the AHA messages from this book socially by going to
http://aha.pub/ACarpentersGuide.

Section II

Good Morning!

The way we start our morning greatly impacts the entire day. If we begin our day thinking that it's going to suck, then it will. The opposite is also true; if we begin the day thinking that it'll be a great day, then it will.

Affirmations can help us start the day right; they're simple, positive things we can say to ourselves every day, such as, "I am a good person," or, "I'm certain that today will be a good day." When we start saying affirmations to ourselves in the morning, we set our minds in a positive state and proceed with our day, focused and determined to make the most of it.

Watch this video:

http://aha.pub/ACarpentersGuideS2

16

If you start your day saying, "Today is going to suck," you're right! If you start your day saying, "Today will be a good day," you're right! What are you saying? #SuccessfulLife

_____

_____

_____

17

Starting off your day with a positive outlook will have a great impact on you throughout the day. Successful people start their day positively. Do you? #SuccessfulLife

_____

_____

_____

18

Start your day saying something positive that your mind will actually believe. #Affirmations change your day for the better. #SuccessfulLife

_____

_____

_____

19

An affirmation is a belief put into words and repeated to yourself with conviction. Affirmations are a great way to begin your day.

_____

_____

_____

20

One way to make your day a good one is to start it off by saying, "Hey, let's begin the day on a positive note." #SuccessfulLife

_____

_____

_____

21

You will meet a lot of negative people at work, which is why you need to use affirmations and say good things to yourself to keep going. #SuccessfulLife

_____

_____

_____

22

Each day brings new challenges, and the negative
person you meet is that challenge. Successful
#Carpenters overcome challenges by thinking positively.
#Affirmations #SuccessfulLife

_____

_____

_____

23

Repeating affirmations may seem silly at first, but not
when you start to believe them and form a positive
outlook on life. What affirmations are you
telling yourself? #SuccessfulLife

_____

_____

_____

24

A positive outlook is essential for achieving a #SuccessfulLife, for without it, you will lose heart and become discouraged. #Affirmations #Carpenters

_____

_____

_____

25

Don't say that you can't do it. If you say that,
you've already knocked yourself out of the game.
#SuccessfulLife

_____

_____

_____

26

#Affirmations reinforce the good stuff in your life.
There's plenty of negative out there. What do you
want more of? #SuccessfulLife

_____

_____

_____

27

#Affirmations help you have a much better outlook on life, a much better time at work, a much better desire to make your goals happen, and a much better chance at a #SuccessfulLife. #Carpenters

_____

_____

_____

28

Use the time you have while traveling to set your mind positively. Listen to positive tapes and interesting audio books. #SuccessfulLife

_____

_____

_____

29

Think of your life as a jar. You can fill it with good
stuff or bad stuff. What do you want in your jar?
#SuccessfulLife

_____

_____

_____

30

When you fill your life with positivity, you get away from
the negativities in the world and become more focused
on attaining a #SuccessfulLife. #Carpenters

_____

_____

_____

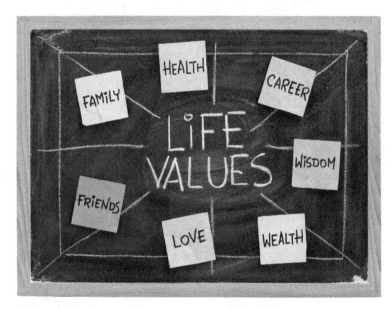

Karl D. Hughes

http://aha.pub/ACarpentersGuide

Share the AHA messages from this book socially by going to
http://aha.pub/ACarpentersGuide.

Section III

The Importance of Values

The values we live by define who we are as a person. Some people may push their own values and beliefs on us, so it's important to be true to ourselves and have a strong hold on our own values to keep moving forward on our path.

We take our values wherever we go, even to our jobs. That's why having a good set of values is what will pave our way and guide us on our journey toward success.

Watch this video:

http://aha.pub/ACarpentersGuideS3

31

No matter what you want to do in life, always ask why you want to do it. Your #Values will guide you on your journey toward a #SuccessfulLife. #Carpenters

_____

_____

_____

32

Your WHY will be the reason you get up, go off to work, and achieve a #SuccessfulLife. What's your why? #Carpenters

_____

_____

_____

33

Motivation is not really taught in school; you need to find that for yourself. What motivates you to do a job?
#SuccessfulLife

_____

_____

_____

34

Successful people go to a job with a plan and a purpose vs. going to a job for money. What are you working on?
#SuccessfulLife

_____

_____

_____

35

You don't do your trade just for money, you do it because you love it. #SuccessfulLife

_____

_____

_____

36

If you're a genuinely good human being, wealth will not change who you are. Don't be afraid of success. #SuccessfulLife

_____

_____

_____

37

Your #Values shape who you are as a person and guide
you on your journey toward a #SuccessfulLife.
What values do you live by? #SuccessfulLife

_____

_____

_____

38

Live your life based on YOUR #Values,
not those of others. #SuccessfulLife

39

Let go of petty prejudices to speed up your
opportunities for success. #SuccessfulLife

40

It's not really justified to be angry or bitter toward someone who is successful, because it doesn't do anything good for you. #SuccessfulLife

_____

_____

_____

41

When you fill your life with negativity, it takes up valuable space where your drive and ingenuity should be. It's in the way of your success. #SuccessfulLife

_____

_____

_____

42

Take pride in your work and who you are. You are your own best supporter. #SuccessfulLife

_____

_____

_____

43

When you wonder how things work and you are in awe of ideas, you become more invested in making things happen. #SuccessfulLife

_____

_____

_____

44

Have a sense of #Wonder. Just thinking about something as simple as putting materials together to build a cozy home can get you motivated to work. #SuccessfulLife

_____

_____

_____

45

#Curiosity is key to learning something new. Are you curious? #SuccessfulLife

_____

_____

_____

46

#Resourcefulness is working with what you have and using it efficiently. Successful #Carpenters are resourceful. Are you? #SuccessfulLife

_____

_____

_____

47

Always strive to do a better job than before. Challenge yourself! #SuccessfulLife

_____

_____

_____

48

If you are in a bad situation, you need to evaluate how you got there and the decisions you made that caused it. #SuccessfulLife

_____

_____

_____

49

#Resilience is sticking with something, no matter what. A resilient #Carpenter still works despite a cold, windy day. Are you resilient? #SuccessfulLife

_____

_____

_____

50

Some of the highest-paid #Carpenters work in very rough conditions. It's not all fine fancy work. #Resilience #SuccessfulLife

---

51

#SelfDiscipline is where you devote enough attention and focus to get something done. Successful #Carpenters have to discipline themselves enough to learn and practice a skill. #SuccessfulLife

---

52

If you are not willing to perform in a job, it's unreasonable to expect the one who hired you to pay you for non-performance. #Discipline #SuccessfulLife

_____

_____

_____

53

#Discipline is a form of love. If you love what you're doing, you discipline yourself to stay with it and practice over and over to get great results. #SuccessfulLife

_____

_____

_____

54

In school, #Discipline means punishment. In reality, it's a key to a #SuccessfulLife. #Carpenters

_____

_____

_____

55

Successful people stay focused on what they want to accomplish. Do you practice #SelfDiscipline? You should! #SuccessfulLife

_____

_____

_____

BE BETTER THAN YOU WERE YESTERDAY

Karl D. Hughes

http://aha.pub/ACarpentersGuide

Share the AHA messages from this book socially by going to
http://aha.pub/ACarpentersGuide.

Section IV

Striving to Be Better

As carpenters, we always want to do a great job. But in order to do that, we must learn all we can about our trade. There are many aspects to our jobs, and we may not know all of them. If we want to earn well, we must be dedicated to knowing everything we can about our field and constantly improving our skills.

An excellent carpenter doesn't become excellent overnight; it takes time, effort, patience, curiosity, passion, and dedication to become the best in the trade. Becoming excellent in your career is essential to success because it opens up more opportunities for employment and for advancement. Just for the mindset of success alone, you must become an excellent tradesman or tradeswoman.

Watch this video:
http://aha.pub/ACarpentersGuideS4

56

Are you willing to become the person you need to be in order to live the life you want? #SuccessfulLife

_____

_____

_____

57

Once you pick up tools, you never put them down.
#SuccessfulLife

_____

_____

_____

58

If you want to be paid what you are "worth," you have
to prove what you're worth first. #SuccessfulLife

_____

_____

_____

59

If you want to earn a great wage, you have to be involved, skilled, and dedicated to your trade. #SuccessfulLife

_____

_____

_____

60

Are there any aspects of your job you're not good at? If so, are you working on getting better? #SuccessfulLife

_____

_____

_____

61

Do you have the necessary skills to do your job? Be honest in evaluating your skills. #SuccessfulLife

_____

_____

_____

62

In order to become good at anything and be successful, you mustn't make excuses for what you don't know. #SuccessfulLife

_____

_____

_____

63

A dog with one trick will not make the circus. You need to learn more than one trick. #SuccessfulLife

_____

_____

_____

64

When you don't take accountability for your actions, it prevents you from becoming successful. #SuccessfulLife

_____

_____

_____

65

Doing the same tasks all the time is okay. But to become successful, you have to learn something new every day. #SuccessfulLife

_____

_____

_____

66

If you want to become a really good #Carpenter, you have to embrace the idea of constantly learning everything about your trade. #SuccessfulLife

_____

_____

_____

67

You can do almost anything when you set your mind to it. #SuccessfulLife

_____

_____

_____

68

The basic skills of a #Carpenter should be so well-practiced and routine that you hardly realize you're doing them. How are your basic skills? #SuccessfulLife

_____

_____

_____

72

Schools focus on academics. However, they don't always teach you skills that pay, such as attention to detail, creativity, and logic. #SuccessfulLife

_____

_____

_____

73

Be a team player, be helpful to others. Offer compliments when people do things right. Share tools and equipment when needed. #SuccessfulLife

_____

_____

_____

74

Be willing to do your share of the not-so-good stuff.
#SuccessfulLife

_____

_____

_____

75

Give advice to the younger people, be willing to teach.
#SuccessfulLife

_____

_____

_____

76

Have a minimum of 100 contacts on your cell phone
that could refer you to a job. #SuccessfulLife

_____

_____

_____

77

The great thing about learning a skill is that it doesn't just pay you once, it pays you again and again. Learn skills, skills pay! #SuccessfulLife

_____

_____

_____

78

The more skills you have, the more opportunities come your way. The more opportunities you have, the better your chances for making a #SuccessfulLife.

_____

_____

_____

79

The basic skills of any profession have to be practiced and they have to become routine. #SuccessfulLife

_____

_____

_____

80

No excuses, learn all the fundamentals. You may not use a skill right now, but you will need it on a future job. #SuccessfulLife

---

81

Never make excuses for a lack of proficiency in the fundamentals of your trade. #SuccessfulLife

---

82

Commit yourself to your trade. Don't make excuses for why you're not good at it. #SuccessfulLife

_____

_____

_____

83

Each thing you learn from a job will help you on the next job. #SuccessfulLife

_____

_____

_____

84

If you improve your skills just 1% per week, then in just 2 years, you will be 100% better than you are now! #SuccessfulLife

_____

_____

_____

85

If you improve your skills 2% per week, in just one year,
you'll be 100% better than you are now. Hmmm...?
#SuccessfulLife

_____

_____

_____

86

If you start working on getting better, you will.
#StartNow on your path to success! #SuccessfulLife

_____

_____

_____

If you want to be successful, give people reasons to talk about you in a positive way.
#Reputation #SuccessfulLife

Karl D. Hughes
http://aha.pub/ACarpentersGuide

Share the AHA messages from this book socially by going to
http://aha.pub/ACarpentersGuide.

Section V

Reputation Matters

Reputation is extremely important in blue-collar trades such as carpentry. If our reputation is good, we won't have to put in much time to search for a job because jobs will come to us. The opposite is true: If we have a bad reputation, nobody will hire us.

Our reputation reaches the job site before we do, which is why creating and maintaining a good reputation matters if we want to be successful carpenters. This section presents the eight qualities we should build our reputations on and how these qualities can help us achieve success in our trade.

Watch this video:

http://aha.pub/ACarpentersGuideS5

87

Decide who you are and what you bring to the game as a #Carpenter. What do you want to define you? #SuccessfulLife

_____

_____

_____

88

In the construction industry, your #Reputation is very important. Reputations get to the job site before you do. What sort of reputation do you have? #SuccessfulLife

_____

_____

_____

89

Even with a lot of contacts, if your reputation is not good, what are your chances of getting a referral at all? #SuccessfulLife

_____

_____

_____

90

If your reputation is good, the guy you're working with today may be the one to refer you to a job several years from now. #SuccessfulLife

_____

_____

_____

91

What do you want your #Reputation to be? How would someone describe you to another potential employer? #SuccessfulLife

_____

_____

_____

92

Qualities to build your #Reputation on: 1) Reliable, 2) Trustworthy, 3) Positive Attitude, 4) Integrity, 5) Competent, 6) Knowledgeable, 7) Determined, 8) Assertive #SuccessfulLife

_____

_____

_____

93

Show up for work every day and on time.
Dress properly and be prepared for work.
#BeReliable #SuccessfulLife

_____

_____

_____

94

Be the kind of person others can count on. Do what you
say you'll do. #BeTrustworthy #SuccessfulLife

_____

_____

_____

95

Do your work to the set standard in a timely fashion.
#Integrity #SuccessfulLife

96

Always perform your tasks and do quality work, whether someone is watching or not. #Integrity #SuccessfulLife

---

97

Take ownership of your mistakes, don't blame others.
You're the only one responsible for your actions.
#Integrity #SuccessfulLife

_____

_____

_____

98

Know your trade. Be well practiced at the
tasks necessary to accomplish your work.
#BeCompetent #SuccessfulLife

_____

_____

_____

99

Always seek to know not just what you're doing,
but also the reasons behind it.
#BeKnowledgeable #SuccessfulLife

_____

_____

_____

100

Take classes to go above and beyond the basics.
#BeKnowledgeable #SuccessfulLife

_____

_____

_____

101

Learn as if you had to teach a brand-new,
inexperienced person.
#BeKnowledgeable #SuccessfulLife

_____

_____

_____

102

Set a goal in your mind as to how long it should take
you to finish your task, and try to finish it in that
amount of time. #BeDetermined #SuccessfulLife

_____

_____

_____

103

Resolve to do your job. Let nothing stop you from completing it. #BeDetermined #SuccessfulLife #PositiveAttitude

_____

_____

_____

104

Speak up when you need to. Determine what needs to be done and do it. #BeAssertive #SuccessfulLife

_____

_____

_____

105

Make decisions; be confident in yourself and in your abilities. #BeAssertive #SuccessfulLife

_____

_____

_____

106

Most employers prefer developing someone they know over hiring someone new. Get that edge! #SuccessfulLife

_____

_____

_____

107

With social media, your #Reputation can spread like wildfire. The question is: what kind of reputation would you like to spread? #SuccessfulLife

_____

_____

_____

108

Successful #Carpenters make things happen, that's their value. Do you make things happen? #SuccessfulLife

_____

_____

_____

109

The #Value of who you are, what you do, and how you conduct yourself will attract jobs to you. #SuccessfulLife

_____

_____

_____

110

Be #Valuable. Go above and beyond what is expected of you. #SuccessfulLife

_____

_____

_____

111

If you want to be successful, give people
reasons to talk about you in a positive way.
#Reputation #SuccessfulLife

_____

_____

_____

Don't assume money is going to keep coming tomorrow. It doesn't. Save and invest. #SuccessfulLife

Karl D. Hughes
http://aha.pub/ACarpentersGuide

Share the AHA messages from this book socially by going to
http://aha.pub/ACarpentersGuide.

Section VI

Do the Math

As carpenters, most of us can make a good living with the money we earn. However, there are some folks who don't. The difference between the two is how we handle the money we're getting. What do we do with the earnings?

Our trade is a young person's game. We are getting older by the minute, and we will soon face physical challenges at work. Besides that, there are other factors that can cause us to become unemployed suddenly. What happens if we get laid off? Are we prepared financially?

This section focuses on how important it is to be prepared for rainy days and provides helpful tips on how to be financially stable as carpenters.

Watch this video:

http://aha.pub/ACarpentersGuideS6

112

Working at a trade, you can make a good living, but then you need to know what to do with the money you're getting. #SuccessfulLife

_____

_____

_____

113

The greatest risk to a tradesman is the day he can't physically work, because he won't be able to earn a living. Start preparing ahead of time. #SuccessfulLife

_____

_____

_____

114

#Carpentry is a young person's game. As you go along, you're going to face physical challenges. What's your plan for later? #SuccessfulLife

_____

_____

_____

115

The day you finish a project is the day you can become unemployed. Are you ready for that? #SuccessfulLife

_____

_____

_____

116

All jobs end and you could be laid off tomorrow. Are you prepared if that happens? Successful #Carpenters prepare themselves ahead of time. #SuccessfulLife

_____

_____

_____

117

Build a rainy day account. #SuccessfulLife

_____

_____

_____

118

Don't assume money is going to keep coming tomorrow. It doesn't. Save and invest. #SuccessfulLife

_____

_____

_____

119

Debt comes from spending money now that you haven't earned yet. Be careful with debt! #SuccessfulLife

_____

_____

_____

120

Credit card debt eats away future earnings. Get out of it as quickly as possible. Stop charging, start paying more than the minimum due. #SuccessfulLife

_____

_____

_____

121

You can stay miserable in #Debt, or you can try to get things to go the way you had intended them. The choice is up to you. #SuccessfulLife

_____

_____

_____

122

Do the math. Take a good look at your expenses.
Are you spending too much on unnecessary things?
#SuccessfulLife

_____

_____

_____

123

If you want to set yourself up into a stronger financial
position and a #SuccessfulLife, focus on the needs
more than the wants.

_____

_____

_____

124

You need to eat but you don't need to buy lunch. Just save the money and bring a lunch from home. #SuccessfulLife

_____

_____

_____

125

Try to save something; even if it's only five dollars a week, you want to get into a habit of saving. Are you saving money? You should be! #SuccessfulLife

_____

_____

_____

126

Aim to save 10 percent of your income, but start by saving what you can. It's a bad week when no money hits the bank. #SuccessfulLife

_____

_____

_____

127

Live below your means so there's money to improve your life. Build a rainy day account. Invest. But always pay yourself first. #SuccessfulLife

_____

_____

_____

128

How do you save enough money to make investments?
Get your debts and expenses under control.
#SuccessfulLife

_____

_____

_____

129

Never count money in somebody else's pocket.
It's not yours. Focus on your money, your goals,
and your successes. #SuccessfulLife

_____

_____

_____

130

Put in the time and energy to study investments,
how they work, and be very careful when you invest.
#SuccessfulLife

_____

_____

_____

131

Even if you earn a good living, it's what you do with the
money when you get it that makes the big difference.
What are you doing with the money you have?
#SuccessfulLife

_____

_____

_____

Share the AHA messages from this book socially by going to
http://aha.pub/ACarpentersGuide.

Section VII

Planning for Success

All successful carpenters have one thing in common: They all plan to be successful. Planning is not something we should disregard. Planning starts with writing our goals down. Once we have written down our goals and read them every day, we will want to take action, and then we do.

Planning not only helps us see the success ahead, but it also helps build up our momentum to actually take action and accomplish our goals.

Watch this video:

http://aha.pub/ACarpentersGuideS7

132

Success doesn't happen by accident. Successful people #PlanForSuccess. Are you planning? #SuccessfulLife

_____

_____

_____

133

The secret to accomplishing goals is to write them down, put them in order, and take action. #PlanForSuccess #SuccessfulLife

_____

_____

_____

134

Write out all your goals on paper. Once you write them
down, they become a part of you. #SuccessfulLife

_____

_____

_____

135

When you are ready to set your goals and start working on them, things will reveal themselves to you that you didn't see before. #SuccessfulLife

_____

_____

_____

136

Set goals. Write them down. Put them in order of priority. And once you do that, it becomes clear as to what you need to do right away. #PlanForSuccess #SuccessfulLife

_____

_____

_____

137

Writing down a goal not only allows you to envision success at the end of the road, it also focuses your attention to actually achieve it. #PlanForSuccess #SuccessfulLife

_____

_____

_____

138

Someone else's success doesn't hurt you. In fact, it could help if you learn from their successes. #SuccessfulLife

---

139

If you read your plans each day, you will focus on the steps you need to take. Even if you do little steps, it will make a difference and you will ultimately achieve a #SuccessfulLife. #PlanForSuccess

---

140

Planning is one of the keys to a #SuccessfulLife.
Discipline yourself to work on your plans.
#PlanForSuccess

_____

_____

_____

Appendix

Affirmations: Some examples of good affirmations, a great way to start your day.

- I am a good person.
- I do my best every day.
- I care for my family wisely.
- Each day brings new wonderful challenges.
- I have a good life.
- Each day brings me closer to my goals.
- I'm good at what I do.
- I'm an excellent carpenter.
- I'm becoming a better carpenter (or other tradesman).
- I use my talents and skills for good use.
- I use my time wisely.
- I am always improving my skills.
- I always make good use of my money.
- Happiness is a part of my personality.
- I am getting there.
- It is very satisfying to do what I do for a living.

Important things that are not taught in schools:

- Attention to detail
- Creativity
- Logic
- Critical thinking
- Resilience
- Motivation
- Persistence
- Curiosity
- Question asking
- Humor
- Endurance
- Reliability

- Enthusiasm
- Civic mindedness
- Self-awareness
- Self-discipline
- Empathy
- Leadership
- Compassion
- Courage
- Sense of beauty
- Sense of wonder
- Resourcefulness
- Spontaneity
- Humility

Qualities to build your reputation on:

1. Reliable

- Show up for work every day.
- Show up on time (at least 15 or 20 minutes early).
- Show up dressed properly.
- Show up prepared.

2. Attitude

- Be positive; there's enough negative out there already.
- Look to contribute to the success of the project.
- Go to work for the outcome, as well as your income.
- Incorporate a strong work ethic.
- Look to be a productive member of a team.
- Have a "can do" approach to all you do.

3. Trustworthy

- Be the kind of person who can be counted on.
- Do what you say you will do.
- Be honest.

4. Integrity

- Do the work to the set standard in a timely fashion.
- Always perform your tasks whether someone is watching or not.
- Do quality work.
- Put the job first, it's why they are paying you!
- Give the employer value for the wages he is paying.
- Take ownership of your mistakes, don't blame others.

5. Competent

- Know your trade.
- Be well practiced at the tasks necessary to accomplish your work.
- Hand skills are essential.
- Basic principles are essential.

6. Knowledgeable

- Always seek to know not just what you are doing but also the reasons behind it.
- Look to learn the next steps in the process.
- Strive to learn all you can about your field.
- Complete all the basic classes on time (or complete your apprenticeship on time).
- Take additional classes to go above and beyond the basics.
- Learn as if you had to teach a brand-new, inexperienced person.

7. Determined

- Resolve to do your job and let nothing stop you.
- Focus on accomplishing the task assigned to you.
- Set a goal in your mind as to how long it should take you, and try to finish in that amount of time.

8. Assertive

- Speak up when you need to.
- Determine what needs to be done and do it.
- Make decisions.
- Be confident in your abilities.

Quick tips from Karl D. Hughes:

- Guard your health at all costs!
- Take $20 (one $10 bill and two $5 bills) and put them in your wallet. Use this for when you are stuck. Cash is always good.
- Pack your bag the night before you go to work.
- Always carry a spare tape measure and some pencils in your bag.
- It is always a good idea to have a small notebook and a pen.
- Always give yourself extra time! There is no perfect commute.
- Remember that there is always another job.
- Don't ever be afraid to sing at work, and laugh too!
- Listen to others.
- Avoid negative people (at all costs).
- Be patient with others if they are not "getting" something.
- Walk with a purpose.
- Bring lunch from home.
- Save all the change in your pocket and use it for vacation money.
- Have a hobby and enjoy it!
- Be respectful to others, it promotes respect for you.
- Know that you can't fix stupid. Stop trying.
- Helping out newer folks helps you.
- Wear a hat and t-shirt when it's hot. Both of these will help keep you cool.
- Best thing to quench a thirst on a hot day is cold water with a sliced-up lemon (or lime).
- Mark out important days on a calendar (like vacations and kids' graduations) and look forward to them.
- Be grateful. For everything. Start with the breath you draw!
- Be valuable. Go a little above and beyond what is expected.
- Focus on the task at hand.
- Use your smart-ass phone as a tool instead of a source for entertainment.

- Let go of petty prejudices, it speeds up your opportunities for success.
- Know that "time spent" is the best present you can give your loved ones.
- Do "Flowers on Fridays." Just give her flowers on a random Friday.
- If you constantly argue with others, remember it is hard to tell who is more stupid.
- It is your right to complain, but whining is not allowed, and nobody listens to complaints, anyway.
- Good strong leadership makes any job great!
- Very often, the lazy guy will know the easiest way to do something.
- Stand back and look at a job well done. Be proud of it.
- It is always great to be able to stand up, go out, and do a physical job.
- Once you pick up tools, you never put them down.
- Sometimes the best thing in the world is to be laid off.

Fending off negativity: They say/you say

Unfortunately, many come into the trades because of a lack of interest in other areas, and then they are working only for a paycheck. They become disillusioned with working hard at a trade.

When they say: "This trade sucks!"

Your answer should be: "Can you tell me anywhere else where given your experience, talent, and education, you would earn the same or more money?"

Usually, they will get angry.

But if they say yes, then you say: "So why aren't you over there?"

They say:	You say:
Get out while you can.	This is my chosen career. I will make it work.
It's not who you know, it's who you blow.	Yes, networking is important.
We don't make enough money.	Actually, we are paid well.
You should go to college instead.	(I have, I like this) or I choose to do this.
Wait till the recession comes.	I am preparing for that now.

Afterword

Now that you have read the book . . .

Use this book over and over like you use a good tool. Go back and mark out which ideas appeal to you the most. Interact with the videos and web stuff. Take notes if that helps you. Write down your favorite tips or affirmations, and place them where you will see them often. Use everything in the book to make your life better.

If there is something you don't agree with, that's okay, don't worry about it. Just go ahead with those ideas that make the most sense right now. Sometimes later on, you will view an idea differently, and then at that time, it will make more sense to you. The important thing is to do something that will help improve what you are doing right now.

About the Author

Karl D. Hughes is a teacher, mentor, and speaker who uses his unique background and knowledge to motivate others to personal, professional, and financial success. Karl's forty-plus years of construction industry experience (master carpenter, business owner, union member, and trade instructor) give him a fresh perspective on goal setting and using one's own skills to succeed. He has a keen ability to communicate his passions to others.

As a sixth-generation carpenter, Karl believes that construction and other blue-collar trades are overlooked as vital and rewarding careers, and he encourages others to explore these opportunities. Karl has a passion for life and learning that he seeks to spark in all those around him.

THiNKaha has created AHAthat for you to share content from this book.

- ⮑ Share each AHA message socially:
  http://aha.pub/ACarpentersGuide
- ⮑ Share additional content: **https://AHAthat.com**
- ⮑ Info on authoring: **https://AHAthat.com/Author**

9 781616 993283